The De

Joanne Hardy

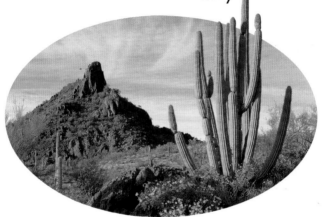

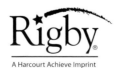

Rigby

A Harcourt Achieve Imprint

www.Rigby.com
1-800-531-5015

Look at the rock.

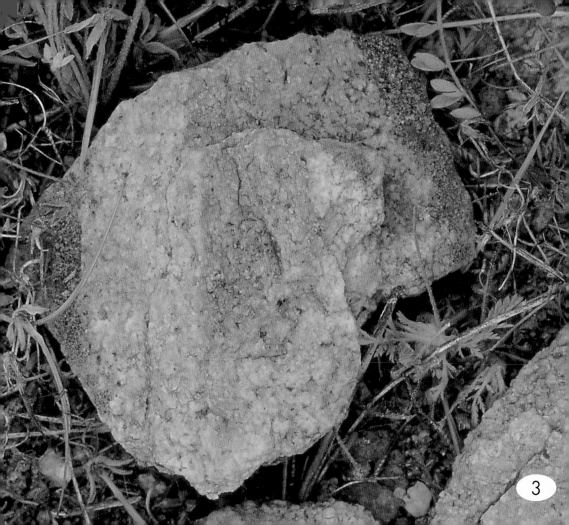

Look at the flower.

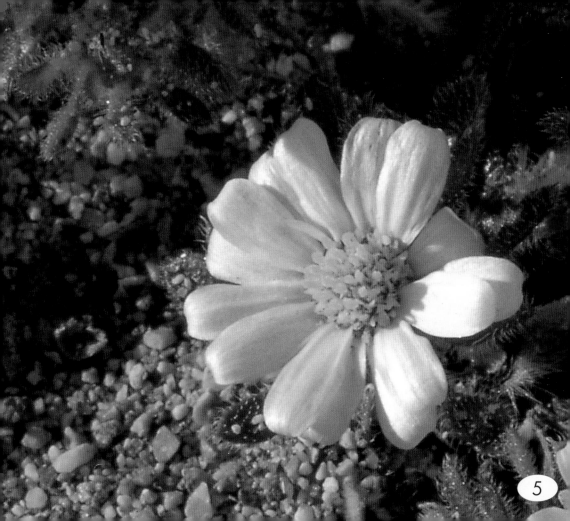

5

Look at the cactus.

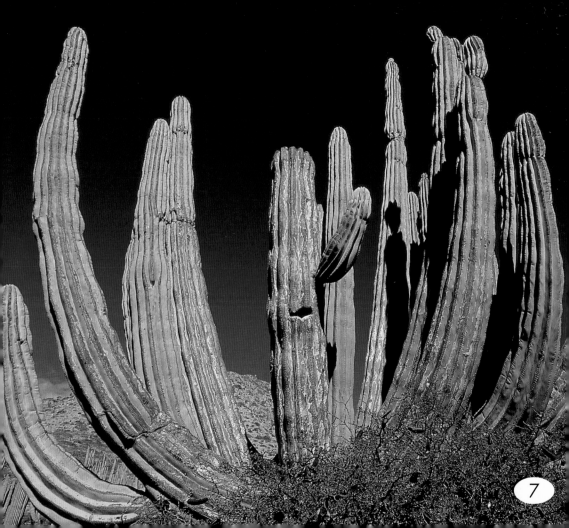

Look at the bird.

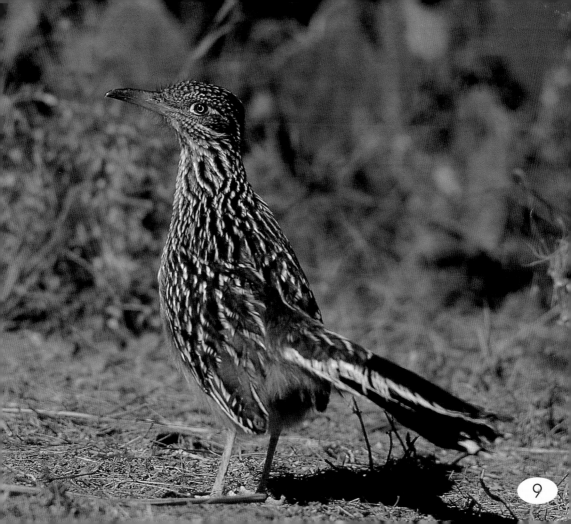

Look at the lizard.

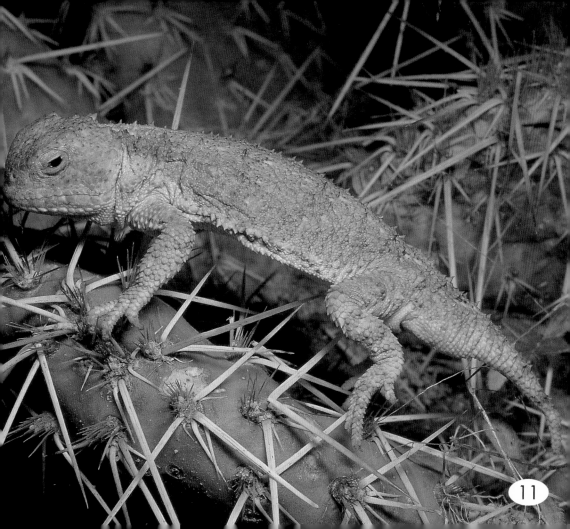

Look at the spider.

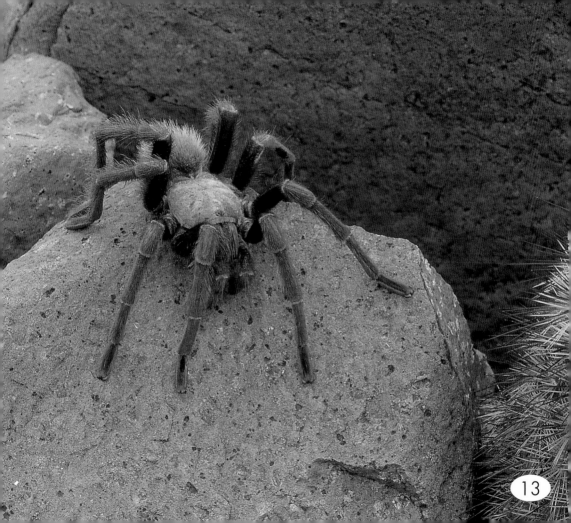

Look at the snake.

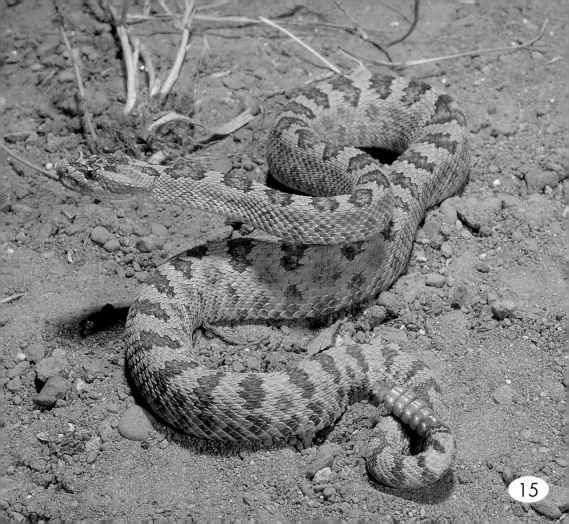

Look at the desert.

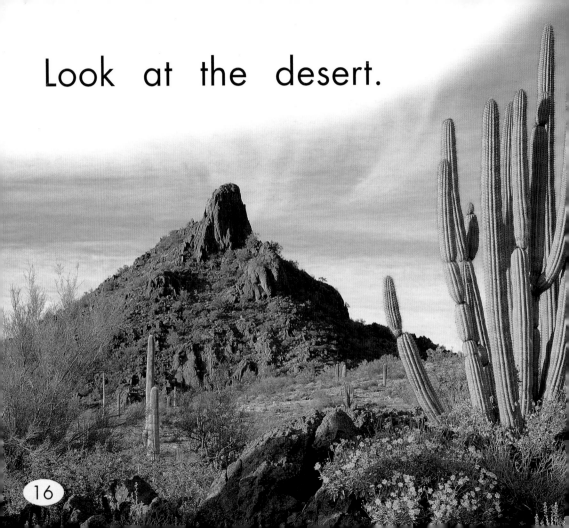